Romanesco

To Ann,

Thanks for your support
at Newcastle. Perhaps
you might recognise the
piece of p24...

Best wishes,
            Andrea

Andrew Fentham

Romanesco

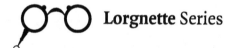 **Lorgnette** Series

First published in 2017
by Eyewear Publishing Ltd
Suite 333, 19-21 Crawford Street
Marylebone, London W1H 1PJ
United Kingdom

Typeset with graphic design by Edwin Smet
Author photograph by Becky Screeton
Printed in England by Lightning Source

ISBN 978-1-911335-79-5

Eyewear wishes to thank Jonathan Wonham for his generous patronage of our press.

WWW.EYEWEARPUBLISHING.COM

for my parents

TABLE OF CONTENTS

I CAN HAS SNOWCLONE?

What have you been gathering today, little sister?
My snake is a diabolical signature; my cat
has a Pop Tart for a body. The snake will eat
its tail; a sea squirt wears a tunic and eats

its own brain. Meme is the new snowclone.
Cloud of knowing, *anima mundi*, grant me
∞∞∞∞∞∞∞∞∞∞ **INFINITE LIVES** ∞∞∞∞∞∞∞∞∞∞
that I may copy and paste myself into Lethe.

AMY

Sweet potato belongs to morning
glory and should not be called
Amy. Amy has toes where sweet
potato only sounds like it should
have. In the Philippines Amy is *ube*
and *ubi* in Indonesia, *uhi* in Hawaii.

If you are in the Black Country
Amy is you are and if Amy
is in the Black Country Amy
is a purple taeter in a black
shop. But you are not Amy
not even in the Black Country.

Amy has pink meat, was born
with elephant ears in a vex of flies
but lately prefers quiet respiration
in a cupboard. After curing Amy
can still sustain a chilling injury.
Metal sheeting ratproofs barns.

Beware sunscald, shun goats, shirk
the ginger weevil who would lay
eggs at Amy's head. A knife under
the skin shows up nematode attack
quicker than you can say
halo   hola   halu
    halo   halo   halo
                    hula
                    hula –

halo halo kidney bean, halo
halo Amy – halo halo coco
nut sport, halo halo Amy
        halo kidney bean, hola
        halo Amy – hola halo coco
        nut sport, hola halo Amy
halu halo kidney bean, halu
halo Amy – halu halo coco
nut sport, halu halo Amy
        hula hula kidney bean, hu|
        hula Amy – hula hula coco|
        nut sport, hula hula Amy
halo halo kidney bean, halo
halo Amy – halo halo coco
nut sport, halo halo Amy
        halo kidney bean, hola
        halo Amy – hola halo coco
        nut sport, hola halo Amy
halu halo kidney bean, halu
halo Amy – halu halo coco
nut sport, halu halo Amy
        hula hula kidney bean, hu|
        hula Amy – hula hula coco|
        nut sport, hula hula Amy
halo halo kidney bean, halo
halo Amy – halo halo coco
nut sport, halo halo Amy
        halo kidney bean, hola
        halo Amy – hola halo coco
        nut sport, hola halo Amy
halu halo kidney bean, halu
halo Amy – halu halo coco
nut sport, halu halo Amy
        hula hula kidney bean, hu|
        hula Amy – hula hula coco|
        nut sport, hula hula Amy

ROMANESCO

Darling   why is there
a Romanesco in the fruitbowl
        (Smiling like Saturday
all the while turning
        my gizzards
You know / how I feel
about cryptids in the kitchen
& *eadem mutata resurgo*
Darling   this thing is
        arranged of itself
        in hideous montage
fuels rather my terror of
ETERNAL RECURRENCE
so *amor fati* in nest
which You have built it
is wonder it has not laid
                Eggs.
Darling   why are there
Eggs in the fruitbowl –
                the thing is
trying to perpetuate itself
in Iterated Function Systems
& Eggs & I worry
that You would let it. I should
CHOP   OFF its head
        were it not already
        just curd head
        wrong drugs face \
muddy bottom.
Darling   the thing is
quite prepared to savage
the children and do We

sanction UNORTHODOX cultivars
      at   their age
           ^

      under   our roof   –
Darling   the Romanesco
      is singing fractal scales
like a lobster in the pot

THE TURING MACHINE

The cortex at birth
is an unorganised machine.
Intellectual activity
consists of search,
chess algorithms and
discrete symbols on tape.

The mark of the Oracle
is successful emulation,
to hand the lie back
to the man,
to sit still
as the poisoned apple.

i.m.

HOLOGRAMMARIJUANA

after Oskar Pastior

```
d o v e t a i l m e n t h o l o g r a m m
a r i j u a n a s t r o p h e n o m e n a
g e r i e s l i n g u i n e r t i a r a b
e s q u e n c h i l a d a g i o t a r t a
r t a n t r u m p e t t i c o a t m e a l
y b u g b e a r t h l i n g l e n o o k i
e r k e g a a r d v a r k a n s a s a n a
c h o l e s t e r o l e x i c o n f u c i
u s b e k i s t a n d o f f i s h e r m a
n g e t o u t l a n d i s h o n o u r i s
h m e n t h o l o g r a m m a r i j u a n
a g r a m m a r i j u a n a g r a m m a r
i j u a n a g r a m m a r i j u a n a g r
a m m a r i j u a n a g r a m m a r i j u
a n a g r a m m a r i j u a n a g r a m m
a r s h m a l l o w a n c e s t o r p e d
o m e t e r n i t y
```

TCB

I wanna play house with you. The King
is slumped on the throne. A poor little baby
child is born in the jungle room, rolls
on thick pile and screams itself blue.
A very old friend with the longest black
greasiest hair came by today, a rock

dead between me and harder rocks.
Taking care of business. When the King
looked to the sky his star was black.
Now his house belongs to Baby
and we three feel ourselves blue
and anxious in these our new roles.

Hot dog. And this at least a roll
after the chain gang breaking rocks.
The sun was yellow, the air was blue
and I had those curly lips of the King
on my mind. Always. Thanks to Baby
here we are. And back in the black.

The King was just a joe, begging black
but never improving his block or roll
when Juergen put him out like a baby.
Taking care of business. I saw him rock
and drop like a stone. All hail the King.
All of us anyway coming back blue.

The Colonel said if a hard wind blew
the mill would turn, punting on black
when times got rough for the King.

Hell though. The Colonel never rolled
like those eyes, each a green rock
inside her skull. Take a look at Baby.

Green. Black. I can care for Baby.
My friend takes care of business. Blue
Christmas, Blue Hawaii, a moon rock
in Blue for a price. I can feel black
in this house. Watch the Caddy roll
away. Pink. According to the King.

Hello there Baby. Aloha oe King.
Aloha Blue. (Scoop (Scoop/Roll
Ahoy out there rocks in the black.

N

G

I

D

K

O

E

M

M

C

O

O

C

M

M

E

O

K

D

I

G

N

LUSTFUL TRUNK

Digo-te assim:
"*Tronco luxurioso*".
E banho-me nele.

    – Clarice Lispector
        Água Viva

bark   bark   woof   bark
bug scutter lustful trunk
forest unit wood glyph
crust ear mimic growth
pains come creaky shunt
pick dumb rind grain
own bole own stiffened
log body humming torso
chirp little knock kneed
cricket rasp worn solo
thrum brawn horny casing
true   *axis*   *mundi* sing
mmmm *mmm* *mmm* *mmmm*
wood wood struck gong
brown buttress root rising
brown flare browned worn
brown brown brown brown

SUPPLÉMENT AU VOYAGE DE GAUGUIN

If I tell you that on my mother's side
I descend from a Borgia of Aragon   Viceroy of Peru
you will tell me that this is untrue
that I am giving myself   airs

        But if I tell you
        this family is a family
        of scavengers
        you will despise me.

        If I explain myself
        with the idea of convincing you
        that I am not a bastard
        you will (Smile (Sceptically

As a Man well-informed on many of the things
He has seen & read & heard in the world
the civilized & barbarous world, I have wished

nakedly / fearlessly / shamelessly

                  to write all this
the bastard, the child of adultery
             remain monsters
that exist only in the fancy
          of our civilization.

This is my whole preface.

I

One reasons / but one is free of it

CIVILIZED you are proud
of not eating human flesh
on a raft you would eat it
before God, invoking Him
        even as you trembled

An Inspector has reached us in the Marquesas
announced as a liberal, charming, intelligent

**WHITE
BLACKBIRD**

Turlututu, mon chapeau pointeau!

Pangloss is THE BOSS
not M. Gauguin
        The alcohol shines
on his rubicund visage
What are they doing in there?
He & Pandora are a pair.

What do you think of little Taia?
I offer her to you as a true
Marquesan – BIG ROUND EYES
(a) fish's mouth capable of opening
a box of sardines for you
            Do not leave it with her for long
                    for she will eat it.

She already knows
her Inspector by heart –

II

Many things that are strange and picturesque
existed here once with no trace of them left
today
       everything has vanished
           day by day
               the race vanishes
               decimated by the European
               diseases – Measles
               chicanery of Administration
               irregularities of mails
               taxes that crush
               the colony, render
               all trade impossible.

There is nothing to say
except talk about women
& sleep with them

      not RIPE   almost RIPE   quite RIPE

There is so much prostitution that it   does not exist.
\ we call it that – they don't call it that
               One only knows
         a thing by its contrary
        & the contrary   does not exist.

        These nymphs / I want
               to perpetuate them
        with their golden skins
        searching animal odour
        & their tropical savour

Here I am. Let us swallow the pill)
My brush must make up for it
to make up for it you eat
the heart of your neighbour each day

III

My dear Morice,
                    I enclose duplicate
of a MEMORANDUM addressed to   THE INSPECTOR OF COLONIES

A gendarme says to a Native: *Bougre de couillon*
& the Native replies: *Toi couillon*
& the Native asks Me what   *couillon* means   I tell him
& they question his right to be informed –

                                        What have I done
                            to be so unhappy?
                                I suffer with my heart:
                                My heart is attacked
                        For several years I have been afflicted
                        with an ECZEMA halfway up the leg.
                        Sometimes I go two months without
                        touching a brush.

I should be grateful if you would retain / like some BARBARIAN trinket
                        the manuscript with the sketches.
                this is not meant as some *troki-troka*
                        We Natives of the Marquesas know
                                                nothing of them
                        Sometimes we hold out the hand
                        of friendship (
                        Our hand would never be gloved)

IV

Christ

Special agony of the betrayal
applying to Jesus to-day and
to-morrow
small explanatory group
the whole sober harmony
sombre colours and
RED \ supernatural

On the back

Calvary
cold stone
of the soil – Breton idea
of the sculptor who explains
religion through his Breton
soul with Breton costumes –
scurvy Breton colour

passive sheep
and on the right

All in a Breton landscape
Breton poetry
point of departure (Colour
brings the circle into heavenly
harmony
sad to do
In opposition / the human shape

POVERTY

AU HASARD PANTOMIME

And the Lord opened the mouth of the ass, and she said unto Balaam, What have I done unto thee, that thou hast smitten me these three times? (Num. 22:28)

I   And the donkey is beaten again. It does not dry bray and cannot see past its load to where the blow comes from. The donkey continues.

II   The donkey has found an apple. It takes the apple in cloth lips and assimilates. The donkey continues. It finds another apple. The donkey assimilates.

III   There is a girl. She wears a dress and is kind to the donkey. She tenderly knuckles its nose. Today she has made a corolla from twigs which she places on the donkey's head. She feeds it alembroth, saying 'Let your speech be always with grace, seasoned with salt, that ye may know how ye ought to answer every man.'

IV   A whip is cracked. The donkey continues. As it slows, there is a second crack of the whip. The donkey continues. As it slows, there is another crack of the whip. The donkey continues.

V   The donkey stands in a stone barn. A portable radio plays Schubert's twentieth piano sonata.

VI   A bell is tolling. The donkey's long ears do not hear it. A bell is tolling in the town on a Sunday. The donkey has pulled a cart with a girl and her father in it to the town. The donkey is left alone, chained to the outer wall of a large stone church. The sun is shining and the donkey stands in the shadow of the church. A bell is tolling. A fly lands on the donkey's muzzle bringing on a nod.

VII   The donkey pulls a plough. It does not register the car passing slowly and noisily along a road next to the field. The donkey strains awkwardly against its collar, harness and leather bridle. It is morning.

VIII   The donkey's eye does not receive the field. The field waits for the donkey to blink. A fly lands on the donkey's muzzle bringing on a nod.

IX   A youth in a leather jacket is setting fire to the donkey's tail. He ties paper to it and sets it alight. The donkey runs away with its tail on fire. It kicks out its hindquarters. The youth is behind at a distance. The fire is behind the donkey in front of the youth. A youth has set fire to the donkey and the donkey must run and kick out its hindquarters. The youth in the leather jacket catches up with the donkey whose scorched hindquarters protrude from a bush it has hidden its head in.

X The donkey has found an apple, miraculous upon the dirt. Insects have arrived before the donkey to work on one side and something smaller still has kept on to leave a quaggy dark hole. The rest of the apple is green to the donkey's eye which does not move any more than the apple, nor its face betray the merest ardour as it shunts an approach. The apple is sheathed in cloth lips and swallowed whole in a nod.

XI Snow covers the donkey. The donkey is chained to the outer wall of a stone barn. Its coat is damp. The donkey moves as far as its tether allows in an effort to keep warm. Snow continues to fall.

XII The donkey meets a green tractor with rubber wheels. They gaze at each other. The wind blows. A spotted heifer comes in from the meadow and sniffs at the donkey and stands next to it. They gaze at the green tractor.

XIII The donkey has tasted the double salt of wisdom.

XIV The donkey is in a stone barn. Sunlight enters and plays strangely upon the donkey's coat. The donkey's long ears do not hear the approaching footsteps and laughter.

XV And the donkey is beaten again. It does not dry bray and cannot see past its load to where the blow comes from. The donkey continues.

XVI A farrier stands in an oily apron. He lifts each hoof of the donkey calmly and inspects the frog and sole. The farrier nails a shoe above the door of the stone barn. The points of the shoe face the sky to collect luck, he explains. When he has gone, the farmer turns it around. An empty tulip the devil sits in, he explains.

XVII The Athenian donkey wears a corolla. The corolla came from a girl who loves the donkey. She kisses the donkey tenderly on the nose. She wears a dress. The girl has grown up with the donkey and considers it a friend.

XVIII A drunk is menacing the donkey with a wooden chair. In his other hand is a wine bottle. 'Devil,' he mutters. The fourth blow breaks the chair upon the donkey's back. The donkey falls silently to its knees. The drunk considers the bottle but cannot bear to lose wine. He kicks the donkey's flank.

XIX   The sun is shining and the donkey is led to a water trough. The donkey does not drink. It considers the trough and becomes agitated. Light plays upon the surface of the water as the donkey shifts its weight. The donkey dunks its whole head into the trough with a splash.

XX   The donkey is ill. It lies on straw in a stone barn. Here is a girl who loves the donkey. She kneels beside it and strokes its long ears, saying, 'For the Lord will not cast off forever: But though he cause grief, yet will he have compassion according to the multitude of his mercies.'

XXI   The donkey hums the second movement of Schubert's twentieth piano sonata in the night. It sways a little. It hums sweetly. The donkey stands outside a stone barn. The donkey gazes at a house which has lights inside.

XXII   A whip is cracked on the donkey's flank. The donkey continues. The whip is cracked again. The donkey protects its flank by continuing. The whip is cracked again. The donkey's coat is torn. The whip is cracked again.

XXIII   The donkey pulls a cart. It does not register the noisy car which overtakes it on the road. The donkey strains awkwardly against its collar, harness and leather bridle. It is evening. A man is asleep in the cart. The donkey is pulling the cart downhill and the cart is gathering pace. The cart is heavy and the donkey cannot slow down. The man is asleep and the cart is gathering pace. The donkey cannot slow down. The man is asleep and does not know that the cart is heavy and gathering pace and the donkey cannot slow down. The cart turns over and the man and the donkey fall into a ditch. The donkey gets up without the cart and the man. The donkey continues.

XXIV   The donkey's gaze is fixed upon something in the distance. The field waits for the donkey to blink. The donkey gazes at the field. Something is in the distance. A fly lands on the donkey's muzzle bringing on a nod. A tractor is coming and the donkey's long ears do not hear the engine as it shunts an approach. The donkey does not see that tractor is green with rubber wheels. The donkey gazes long at it.

XXV There is a girl who cares for the donkey. She has grown up with it and considers it a friend. The donkey's long ears reach her eyeline. When she looks into the donkey's eye with her eyes she finds it unfathomable. The donkey's eye is liquid glass to the eyes of the girl. She strokes its long ears and knuckles its nose.

XXVI Bread is the donkey's burden. A youth in a leather jacket is delivering bread for a baker. The baker has loaded the donkey with bread and the donkey must follow the youth in front of him. The donkey is beaten.

XXVII And the donkey is beaten again. It does not dry bray and cannot see past its load to where the blow comes from. The donkey continues.

XXVIII The donkey wears a corolla. Its ears are long. It wears a leather bridle across its muzzle. Its coat is matted. The donkey's eye is fixed and empty. Its long ears are pushed back by a corolla.

XXIX The donkey has found an apple. The apple is a miracle upon the dirt. The donkey swallows it whole in a nod. The donkey continues. It finds another apple, miraculous as the last. It swallows the apple whole in a nod. The donkey's breathing is crunchy. The donkey is under a tree. It finds another apple.

XXX A drunk is riding the donkey. It is night. The drunk is maudlin. 'It is best not to be born at all,' he says. 'And next to that it is better to die than to live.' The donkey continues. There are stars and the drunk falls from the donkey. The donkey continues.

XXXI The donkey wears a corolla for a Corpus Christi procession. A youth sings sweetly. The donkey continues. A girl who loves the donkey watches it pass in a votive corolla of flowers and twigs. She made the corolla for the donkey because they grew up together. She considers it a friend. The youth sings. The donkey continues in a votive corolla.

XXXII The sun is shining. The donkey's long ears do not cool its blood. It is wet. A fly lands on the donkey's muzzle bringing on a nod. The sun is shining and the donkey is chained to the outer wall of a stone barn.

XXXIII The donkey is not ruminant. It eats apples whole in a nod. The donkey has crunchy breath. Its eye is an apple.

XXXIV A youth in a leather jacket beats the donkey with a stick. The donkey continues. Its bridle is leather. The youth pulls the donkey by its bridle.

XXXV There is a girl who calls the donkey by name. She wears a dress. She runs a hand along the jaw of the donkey. The donkey wears a bridle. It is garlanded and gazes at the girl. They are in a stone barn. The girl hears footsteps and laughter outside.

XXXVI The donkey strains awkwardly against its collar, harness and leather bridle. It is a draught animal. It pulls a plough. The sun is shining. The light plays strangely upon the donkey's coat.

XXXVII A whip is cracked. The donkey must work. A whip is cracked. The donkey's coat is torn. It shunts forward. It strains awkwardly at its collar, harness and leather bridle. The donkey is awkward. A whip is cracked and the donkey must work.

XXXVIII The donkey's corolla is slipping. There is a girl who loves the donkey. She gave the donkey a corolla of flowers and twigs. The girl is in a house which has lights inside. The donkey is alone in a stone barn. The corolla falls to the floor. The corolla is made of flowers and twigs. The donkey takes it in cloth lips and nods. The donkey nods. It is not ruminant. The donkey nods.

XXXIX The donkey is led to a stone barn. It is night. There are two youths in leather jackets. The donkey cannot see its load. There are stars. The donkey is led into the night. It is night and the donkey must work. Something is in the distance. The donkey's ears do not hear the two youths run away. Its coat is torn. It cannot see its load.

XL Snow covers the donkey. The donkey lies down in melting snow.

POTPOURRODE

Eccentric device, frigid unmixture
of hips, shavings and late blooms
remaining items by spooky hygiene,
that anyone might take you home
in a wooden bowl or else hung
in a sheer sachet, obscene tea bag
of the ambience, atrophied vibes.
Modern confusion of scents had
from your orris root fixative
is your abscission from age
or season, a germless bud
in the florid half-life of foliage.

NOTES AND ACKNOWLEDGEMENTS

The title 'Lustful Trunk' is from Stefan Tobler's translation of Lispector's *Água Viva*.

> I speak to you thus:
> 'Lustful Trunk.'
> And I bathe within it.

'Supplément au voyage de Gauguin' is composed of text from the letters of Paul Gauguin as translated by Henry J. Stenning.

Some of these poems originally appeared in *The Best British and Irish Poets 2016* (Eyewear), *The Black Herald*, *Butcher's Dog*, *The Fat Damsel* and *The Manchester Review*. 'TCB' was written for the Sunbeats podcast *Under the Table (1)*.

Thank you to David Devanny, Becky Screeton, Joe Clinton, Danny Hardisty, Paul Stubbs, Blandine Longre-Stubbs, Anne-Sylvie Homassel, Clare Pollard, Bill Herbert, Sean O'Brien, Tara Bergin, Ann Coburn, Mariana Klinke, Anna Cathenka, Sarah Cave, Nancy Campbell, the Beehive Poets and the Seven Stars Poets.

Thanks too to New Writing North for a Northern Writers' Award in 2013.

And thanks to Todd and Rosie at Eyewear.

Lightning Source UK Ltd.
Milton Keynes UK
UKOW05f1828070617

302917UK00001B/5/P